John Doyle

A Stirring At Dusk

For my parents James and Helen Doyle, and to the following for their support and encouragement over the last two years - Ken Folan, Enda Carr, John Greene, Michelle Goddard, Chris McMahon, Niall Weldon, Andrew Clarke, Catherine Mulrennan, Pacelli Doyle, Heather Stewart, Andy Lawless, Irene Matthews, Séamus Carr, Steven Storrie, Grant Tarbard, David Cooke, John Warwick Arden, Alex Dempsey, Shay Claffey, Anthony Smith, Monica Baron, John H. Olson, Daragh Hickey, Eddie Connolly, Ivor McCormack, Rory Nolan, Gerard James Hough, Burt the Dog.

Oh, and of course, God; without whom shit-creek would be my full-time residence.

A selection of these pœms originally appeared (in some shape or form) in A *New Ulster, Clockwise Cat, In Between Hangovers, The Galway Review, Degenerate Literature,* and *Your One Phone Call*

I would like to thank the editors of the above websites and publications for their support and generosity.

This book is dedicated to the memory of Julia Moran (1929 - 2014)

"Dusk time, the shadows fall,
into the timeless time of all"
—The Beach Boys "All This Is That"

"Ní thuigeann an sách an seang"
—Old Irish Proverb

"The life of the dead is set in the memory of the living."
—Cicero

Contents

Man of the Hinterlands

I.M. - John Nolan

Ebullient soil sparkles,
in wind-chime currency
grandfather spent,

those wounded ribbons
weeded from grace,
at the clicking spine of dawn,

and in every truss there is obedience, to this king
who lies in state on my kitchen wall;
miles of kindred

are fingers
caressing his Edwardian pocket-watch,
miles of descendants

a chain of scythes, clicking sparks
on clusters of unblemished stone -
I watch morning rays sparkle on his wedding ring,

a fervid sweat tingle his un-ripened wrist,
more exact than Descartes, he grapples a
burnished sun-flashed hœ, his hinterland currencies called to arms

Animal Magnetism

"...the damned are damned because they enjoy being damned."
Patrick Kavanagh

Her cousins were the nicest folks I've ever met,
sheepdog the size of Norway,
a few ducks running wild,

when her 2nd cousin left the yard-gate open
and the horses galloped like thunder,
it was like they could read minds through time and space,

her eyes flashed like forked lightning,
her fists flapped like hurricanes locking antlers,
and a single colt cleared a buckled fence never to be seen again.

Elderly Woman On the Bus Speaking Russian

A gurgling throat in
familiar tone, snuggles this
endless line,
Kazan winter immeasurably raw, impossible to touch,
there is a glow, a moment that hums
each syllable, indexed on her voice,
on distant ears
they'll huddle, sonic tightrope, defrosted;
it's as if ice shakes beneath eavesdropping birds,
elderly woman,
a plum-cheeked cooing child,
endless line thumping
with this simmer of electric words

Saving an Ant from Drowning

I watched galaxies scurry last week,
as mother and me loosened clay-caked crag,
like teeth the garden lost from tobacco-tanned gums,
we spied histories, a cult of leisure
bashing bumper cars at summer night fairs,
where the queen was the carnie's daughter
flashing her rose-painted lips, as moonshine slid promise on
her skin-tight pants,
their eyes filled gardens like shilling-grey stone;

As I move a frigid coffee, one bobbles for dear life,
like Natalie Wood starstruck in caffeine skies,
my finger dives in, a token of remorse;
I think of the garden this week,
where mothers glow tobacco-brown like sunsets in Mississippi,
empires lost in cold chills of muck,
and the pimple-pressed boys who scurry for summer night
queens;
there will be one who gets away -

Dear Lord, let there always be one

High Noon, Texas Badlands.

The whole town
edged to one side,
blistered light squeezing its frigid day,

in silent depths of space
where wind tickled gorse,
where killers sharpened knives, a tutor for runaway boys;

a kid eyeballed his own ghost
running home to ma with teary-tales,
tales that made hair stand up -

to make an embalmed shadow rise.
They've found rest
from this lung-punching sun,

denim jacket drifter,
the boy who peers around to
spin the roulette wheel once more,

the tin-coffin beans
slashed open,
the frying pan, and coyotes afoot...

The Men Who Built Durrow Viaduct, County Waterford

"God sells us things at the price of labor." — Leonardo da Vinci

Trembling thundering sandstone rolls,
softening, hissing hush of grass,
ice-age had its curators, moving
to a hurried beat of time,
moving as gift to numberless men,
they sired their science patting argent stone,
their welted hands as compass, scribe, and map,
moving, singing, an alignment of shapes,
the bowed bend of mountain crag
jigsawed in time,
men without science, scribes to God and God alone,
the palm-smooth swerve slotted in mountain curve,
cloth caps donned on professorial heads.

Welts

It was my first welt -
October 1993,
earned pumping gas
for some
two-bit huckster down the road,

in night-visions a '51
Chevrolet
would roll in beside my pump,
me, and this God-fearing coot called
Klaus — comparing welts;

he would drive home to Martha, chuckling,
I showing mine to dad,
his knees ascended from winter-scent ditches,
welts the size of Kansas—
mine a prototype, straight from Rhode Island.

Cambridgeshire, 1970

(For David Cooke)

Arise! England's
scents are adrift, in straw-hat whimsy,
as an equinox
aligned to breeze-flicked corn,

our children gather in giggles
and mild-blue bows,
sparkle-tinged cider,
in case fathers drift from shore,

imagine this home-movie glint
as colours fire sparks on screen,
or swollen wheat and June ablaze
in hues of *Eastman* colour,

imagine footprints, fluent fields
with pond-moistened shœs,
the peeling flesh
shedding marrow, from single-crew boats,

the fizz of lawns thrilled
in gold-crest booze -
corn, wheat, a stand of semaphores
to an ale drinker's moon

Baby, Let's Not Play House

Not a breath from the highway as the sky lies flat and bruised,
dawn has shattered neon,
and falling glass at least, brings this acropolis some respite,

I take shore-leave
to find our twisted wreckage everywhere,
sticky wine, ashen narcotics,

and a few forgotten coats -
so much more revealing
minus their animated shapes,

a dangling curtain
blocks these ruins from further shame,
to think, this could have been Valencia - just once more,

the bass-drum thud of falling lemons
and grumpy ex-pat dogs,
who rationed sun for a blessed day...

I slam iron bars behind me
and slot back
in my cold fetal shape,

Sunday's first motion driving past
as Dylan sings of smoking box cars; I watch her husk fill with
death, *Baby*, I sing, *I don't wanna play house with you*

Films of Long Gone Irish Railway Lines

To guess a town's importance -
count how many tiers
telegraph poles had,

wobbling saunter through bog -
two tiers at most -
still room though for budding Flann O'Briens,

tilted fedoras and half-shut macs,
a platform squeezed fag
under life-heavy boots;

their pin-stripe mystery vanishes in circles
of *Third Man* smoke,
as engine enters tunnel

on abruptly snapped reel;
Kafka's stomach -
left acrid and tanned

Matrimonial After-Party

The old man was hammer-blunt,
(and I don't think it was booze this time),
"who are you?" he accused,
the last 20 years
a stagnant radar,
on his Iscariot-etched face.
Merlot blotches assumed their mantle —
let's boogie through another night of war,
though moderate, only words, or lack of, causing any scars,
the groom's jacket off, attending to the vacant and dead.
Spirits meanwhile were howling, some from glasses, some that
shot down
the respite a moment's toast gave,
sunken-eyed
pot-bellied loners mauled oul wans,
twisting their night away.
I thought of the tropics,
for lovers married on a quilted beach, and the only song I
heard was Led Zeppelin's *That's The Way,*

a coroner hardly need decipher,
this ringing microphone fuzz of death

The Antimeridian

There's no doubt
we'll make babies
in a farmhouse b'n'b,

a place where dawn pummels
night, back through sky's suffocating holes;
As we wrap matters up

BBC Radio 4 jump-leads the universe to life,
longwave starlight a fire,
from which God embalms us;

We'll name our child for one -
akhir an-nahr
driest of Arabic plains,

where morning outwits desert sand,
Abu Dhabi a fire-blurred vision,
of neon and traffic squeals,

if it's a girl, then *Bellatrix*, daughter of Orion,
umbilical tightrope to distant ports;
Tony Iommi's intro on *Spiral Architect*

pops babies from morning's stellar womb,

the flesh of lambs tanned in sunrise,
the dew settling on our hands -

like constellations;

The outside is silent,
the spiders' webs engorged
by day, where eyes meet I; You and I.

Corsica

We have marched far enough -
let us concede we are
not pure-blooded Moors,
the sinking of fizzy vapor
by a statue,
is all we can emulate,

our day is serried with olives,
yet our packed guts up their demands,
sò feritu, I cry,
an incumbent challenge
mortified, by map-filled
allegorical streets -

deceived
by the cooling swathe of churches,
doors fastened
between *Holy Spirit*, and the breath reposing on our lives,
rock-face houses that tip further to their death,
a moment's chatter, then headlong descent to sea—

and we shudder at seagulls,
their mortal shrieks
voluble in holes that puncture dental cliffs,
ultramarine,

turquoise,
our quest for respite, patched in tender rubicon of sea

Winter: Fire and Water

i.m. Janet Nolan

As I read my Thomas Merton,
I learn to know the *Christ of the burnt men,*
as I watch crisp leaves flutter,

they spark a boundless sky—

and there she speaks; a prose
the pyres
of winter cannot out-bloom;

When that woman glows in empyrean bronze,
think of Thomas Merton,
his winter charred, fiery elements shocked apart,

think of her -

luminous fire, raptured by sea;
God's seraphic paint breathes cool and warm,
on two warriors' embattled skin

Scarf

Simmering i.d.
on torso,
bless this woman - in your
foremothers' softened needle,
in the clangs of resin, music
for a chilled November sonnet,

bless those black suede ballet pumps,
her insteps wrapped in October's hold,
her lightly-baked shroud
rambling, on diamond-cut rug—
scarf, my dear, hold on;
don't forget her, even if she forgets you

Ag Éisteacht le Mary Bergin—*Feadóga Stáin*

Faoi bhun, tá sé níos boige ná ceol,
Baile Átha Cliath
ag athrú isteach ina Chill Mhantáin -
ag cur báistí arís,
ach báisteach bog,
an áit ina luíonn craiceann
isteach cruthanna sléibhe boga,
ar an mbealach a ghluaiseann sí,
an bean, agus a h-amhrán,
an fuaim cosa fliuch, comharthaí ó mhóin,
1979,
ar an lá seo chonaic muid
na sléibhe ag lasadh go mall, ag canadh go deo...

Petrified Corpse, Los Alfaques, 11th July, 1978

You'll be in Heaven when this horizon melts,
your death-mask seared on miners in '34,
Asturian coal rolled in blood,
as your bones crack like union-men under Franco's ascending foot,

and your blessings too
lie charred in black and white, the scowl,
the nuanced disbelief, the ink of remembrance
those sangrias sipped, by a gutted baptism font,

but as your soot-tint digits accusingly weld, remember Dante's licking
garbs, or *Guernica*'s encore
untamed by useless sea,
your eyes clasped on shrouded teens, huddled by the smoke-cured baths.

Your *danse-macabre* is encircled
by light to moderate showers,
lateness of rain, a tease for pointless police car lights—eyes two moons
on pitch-black skin,
for astrologists to gaze at and weep

The Biscuit Jar

A few were left
when she skimmed home from mass;
her footsteps vivid, impromptu, in her wizardly frame,
every taste was benediction, crumbling from that copious jar,
the fragrance was the wildest scent, of lands she never traipsed,
keenly un-circling
a chiming rim,
she would dream of Moscow, of Tangiers, radios dials where strangers
ghosted cinereal stone, then returned a jar half-full
to the clustered music of her kitchen press.

Look at her now;
hours tightening skin
on a face that
need dream no more,
a lid, soon to close.
I coax that jar now,
sudden artefact that
offers two crowning bites -
one I make sacrament with, to feed a gaggle of wrens,
one I cannot touch - her abiding face whispers *"leave it for me"*,
lid staying un-closed, an epilogue un-scored.

i.m. Kitty Connolly 1936 - 2016

Bad Schandau

The trees swallow sudden pinks,
stretching plump fattened clouds,
the train coasts garden by garden,
the trees rich in breath, hiss light on nude nubile shapes...

The Colours of Death Were Sexier in 1981

One dœs not shoulder much water
for a fist-squeezing *Euro* bottle,
like a child I have been snared,
hook, line, and sinker again -
colour leering on labels, it was always my Achilles Heel,
20 Major smokes in 1981
had a similar nuance of mystery-cradling green,

and I looked at men dying of cancer
in that catacombed Blanchardstown ward,
solar systems of fields outside,
Dublin yet to conquer—
all shielded in *20 Major* packet green;

I grew weary, cœrcing a pallid bottle
on a belching bin,
greener than their retirements of skin, with morbid envy;

An arriving ambulance wailed its blues
on the city's bony fingertips,
sapphire water submerging the green, now abandoned deltas...

One Thing About Weeds

I.M. Mary Doyle 1921 - 2016

"*One thing about weeds*" she would say
"*is that they never forget*"—
on prim and proper soil
come Summer's eve,
their callow needles pricking jibes,

a chattering clique on that heavy breeze;

as I march behind a funeral
I see them choke every nook in town,
taller and taller they rise,
the ugliest chatter
of heads unbowed,

no, those weeds never forget...

I've wiped my mouth,
my bowl bubbles into sink,
as a kitchen door
slams shut behind me,
sun luminous on scythe,

her blood bubbles within me, no, I won't forget...

To An Ex-Boss...
(*The JobBridge Blues Shuffle in 4/4 Time*)

Her asperous drone
latched on each and every thorn
Ulster briers gargled up,
a rolling tumbling jackdaw
tongue,
missing only music
and everything thus,
her *heys* and *highs*
marched with crows to the clasp of day,
voice thinner than chipped mountain flint -
morning's sleet
burning and lashing
from a cackling hawk's
sudden swoop,
her eyes so black
every star
lay dead
behind a tea-bag stained warehouse wall

Santa Teresa De Gallura

There is green, there is black -
evening needs little colour
to impress,
evening's not always the chameleon's whipping boy,
I watch trees dip like emeralds,
dangling moon and sun
through cat-piss streets
where dogs soon take charge,
and every song is a newborn tongue
tracing sounds from forgotten lives,
be it blotches that splinter space
between sea and night,
or the foggy collage of Bonifacio
soon to strike,
on the hill where people made illicit talk—
in *Gallurese, Sardo*, a canvas whispered on
sky-drenched script,
I saunter the greenest leaves, my shadow seared on blackened
lanes of night,
I write with ink moon filled their souls with -
the purple clouds are the storm of words,
where Jesus' blood was tattœed by sunset

Street Lime *(Painting By Eoghan McGrath)*

For seconds
an impasse,
in this billowing wood;

wise money assumes
day-time will try to escape,
no,

perhaps it cried sanctuary,
both entranced,
and firing each russet spark

in every crackle of brown;
every strangeness of being
huddles beneath those chambered limbs -

and what of those trees,
those dank-trellised veins
waiting for a fix,

golden brown,
coffee sunrise,
the shape of hammer-clinked bone

who tells stars' apparitions how ugly they are,
its soot-sprinkled sag an invite,
for sky to seek revenge - all bets called briskly off

Older Brother Types...

Were kept close to us,
not through age, nor kin, only presence
on those hey presto, cigarette cloud walls,

older brothers
could seize metropolis all on their own,
a triumphant puff of weed on the bus, though fetal and alone,

they were always called *Kevin*, wore DMs,
their heads prized-down,
Kevin used x-rated words like "*culture*", while we muttered
a long deceased "*fuck*".

My friend's kin Kevin
looked like he would blow his brains out
not long after 1989,

in 2016 I saw him—
head still down; his dreadlocks were nested in withdrawn silver,
a pram wishing its time future bound, to dad-baiting attitude

and the town's only Mudhoney LP.
I saw Def Leppard seared on every street corner, a sneer of
dead red petals
at his electricity bill-caked feet

The Enterprise Roars Through
Balbriggan Station

Sail away, away/Ripples never come back -
Ripples - Genesis 1976

Chilly waters whisper,
as sea and sand lock lips once more,
like the moon-splashed bride un-gripped her life, from numi-
nous terrain,
Balbriggan, 1-51pm,
ocean jewels me
with tangs of salt, skeletal veils of maritime life, my footprints
are a paper trail
some dogs
rally round, then abruptly discard,
like the *Guinness* breath
of her wayward love,
severed, in blades of Dublin to Belfast fumes

Jogging

People jog this city
after dusk,

late-shift i.t.heads,
killers who flinch -

helpless to fight the urge;
I watch a pair from my bus window,

how often their shœ-prints must pass
in street-lamps of dreams and horror,

caught in real time, the obscured marathons of night -
I'll invite them for coffee,

watch the killer flicker, and twist his Bundy smile,
an i.t. kid and his unearned beard -

they sit frozen,
my fingertips less reasoned than a starting gun;

the pale bones of waitress
centre-stage -

when knives and forks fall,
a race begins

John Cale's Helen of Troy

John Cale's heart slides down his sleeve,
wise move son—
making inroads on Helen of Troy,
my, how sweet that music smells,
shimmering to a rock-steady beat,
an equine ruse wheels down jazz-bar stairs,
clickety-clacks in lovers' swollen heels,
softened only, by Grecian dusk -
their hooves run deep
on sinking scarlet moons,
as they sit naked by that equine ruse,
bridle-free, hair like dawn caught fire,
their love as soft
as strands of night, on sleeping battlefields

Seaweed

Polyphyletic slime, sentient prey,
big rock sleepy, one-eyed
chalky stare, belly of waters, nauseating whiff,
the slaughter of the innocent in shore-side
warning signs, the kamikaze gulls burning
brittle bookend clouds.

You are their murky globular bling,
choose carefully, please

Kontxa Hondartza, Donostia, Iraila 2012

Saturday Night, Sunday Morning

Saturday night
would plummet like Autumn from our lives,

celluloid crisp like auburn leaves,
astrological frames of thick-goggled black.

Remember
Mannix, Parkinson, Hawaii 5-0?

McGarrett sealed a vault behind him -
midnight unplugged, the world spun to a bone-dust spec;

Every screen in the city was breathless,
as freight-train and tomcat became synonyms of black.

Sunday morning was an odd-toothed man—
pulling a key from a hook as he wiped his nose,
his bike chattering against a chapel wall

Pski's Porch Publishing was formed July 2012, to make books for people who like people who like books.
We hope we have some small successes.
www.pskisporch.com.

Pski's Porch

323 East Avenue
Lockport, NY 14094
www.pskisporch.com